THE PORTAGE POETRY SERIES

SERIES TITLES

Bone Country
Linda Nemec Foster

Not Just the Fire
R.B. Simon

Monarch
Heather Bourbeau

The Walk to Cefalù
Lynne Viti

The Found Object Imagines a Life: New and Selected Poems
Mary Catherine Harper

Naming the Ghost
Emily Hockaday

Mourning
Dokubo Melford Goodhead

Messengers of the Gods: New and Selected Poems
Kathryn Gahl

After the 8-Ball
Colleen Alles

Careful Cartography
Devon Bohm

Broken On the Wheel
Barbara Costas-Biggs

Sparks and Disperses
Cathleen Cohen

Holding My Selves Together: New and Selected Poems
Margaret Rozga

Lost and Found Departments
Heather Dubrow

Marginal Notes
Alfonso Brezmes

The Almost-Children
Cassondra Windwalker

Meditations of a Beast
Kristine Ong Muslim

When I Was Baptized in Missouri Dirt

The poems in this wise and moving collection emerge from childhood and from a family farm where cattle drift through trees like "spy satellites," cicadas resemble "live mines," and a septic tank is like a "submarine drydocked" in Missouri. This is the Reagan-era, Cold-War world in which Parmenter goes "echo hunting." This is his "exacting look back." But as I read these exquisitely crafted poems, I realized that they aren't about the past, not ultimately, and that the careful and accurate scrutiny of their gaze unleashes reverberations that reach us here, again and again, with moments of stunning insight and of real beauty.

—DAVIS MCCOMBS
Yale Series of Younger Poets Award Winner
author of *Lore*

In *When I Was Baptized in Missouri Dirt*, Chad Parmenter constructs a child's world of loneliness and terror—including the terror of finding out who you might actually be. He brings to that vision a post-Adamic talent for naming the world's strangeness in phrases heavy with hard-earned knowledge and poetic skill. He describes "the garage door, leaking dark / like a castle wall." In a pile of tin cans he imagines "the air-marrowed / body of a robot." These poems are alive to and in difficult knowledge, and they make mystery articulate without diminishing the dark wonder it contains.

—JONATHAN FARMER
author of *That Peculiar Affirmative*

I can't imagine a better Georgic for our age than Chad Parmenter's *When I Was Baptized in Missouri Dirt*. On one hand, a book about coming of age on a small farm, it is also a book that reaches for God without losing hold of chickens or cicadas. Not since Heaney have I read poetry that speaks with such abundant lyrical freshness.

—RODNEY JONES
National Book Critics Circle Award Winner

When I Was Baptized in Missouri Dirt

poems

Chad Parmenter

CORNERSTONE PRESS
UNIVERSITY OF WISCONSIN-STEVENS POINT

Cornerstone Press, Stevens Point, Wisconsin 54481
Copyright © 2026 Chad Parmenter
www.uwsp.edu/cornerstone

Printed in the United States of America.

Library of Congress Control Number: 2026930827
ISBN: 978-1-968148-29-4

Cornerstone Press titles are produced in courses and internships offered by the
Department of English at the University of Wisconsin–Stevens Point.

DIRECTOR & PUBLISHER   EXECUTIVE EDITORS
Dr. Ross K. Tangedal   Jeff Snowbarger, Freesia McKee

EDITORIAL DIRECTOR   SENIOR EDITORS
Brett Hill   Paige Biever, Eva Nielsen, Reilly Crous

PRESS STAFF
Allison Lange, Karlie Harpold, Kim Janesch, Sophie McPherson, Sam Bjork,
Madison Schultz, Autumn Vine

To Boo

CONTENTS

ECHOSYSTEM

When I Discovered Sacrifice By Fire

There are so many ways
of burning things, but
not many of containing
the flames they become
that last. Our burn barrel,

replaced just often enough,
would hold a year's worth
of fire, or not much more,
before flaking away, not
as ash, but as steel veiled

with so much heat, for so
long, it looked like bark,
but rust-dark, with cracks
like rivers in a magic
map running while dry,

leaking rapids of ash that
was never, in my memory,
actual black or white, but
some frustration of gray
where my never-settling

eyes, with no memory
guiding them, could not
recover what was burnt,
what junk mail brochure,
what bouquet of paper

towels, what white web
of plumage plucked from
chickens in the minutes

after slaughter. Was my
one find in that starburst

of bare dirt, ash-blanched
around the barrel's husk,
my knife that I had lost and
given up on, easily, out
of a sacrificial spirit that

said "no" to what I loved?
It was too molded by fire
to open again, into a thin
little finger, Swiss cross
run up, by fire, as haze

in the smoke that so many
memories rode toward
a fear-conjured, mad God
who never seemed so
close to me as when Dad

pitched a match in, and
fire climbed faster than
we could manufacture,
no faster than it had
for our ancestors, and

any sins got flushed from
the same ash that anyone
burning anything, anywhere
could see, sins gone like
mine might be in Him

who might one day leave
nothing of me. Maybe

it was a flame form of faith,
ragged but dogged, bright
as it was short, that kept

me from reaching in, even
when it held no heat, our
burning barrel, even when
all I could find would be
something to wash away.

Faller

At seven, an Anabaptist with baby fat,
I had some sick love of lacking things,
that way of getting hurt in order to be saved,
of giving way when the slightest crisis hit,
divinely guided to slide like lightning and fall
into the radar, then care, of whatever stood
for heaven just then. I was not God's.
I could only try to signal His angels in.

Anyway, that's my slant on that afternoon
when I ran to the catastrophe of an apple tree
that leaned on the plank top of the fence
dividing our yard from the highway,
dying, no reason to run to it that I knew.

I like to think the scattered, past-ripe apples
made a moldering solar system in its roots,
that the musk of them, half-trampled,
lined the wind, cut the scent of the interstate
where our dog had been run down,

but I can't remember what I wanted there,
just the run up its trunk, crushing away bark
to show the circuitries of termite burrows,
the canopy all bald wood, all rain-grayed,
like a medusa stared at hard by her sister.

I shinnied onto the one branch low enough for me, mighty
and tiny at once, like a tyrannosaur arm,
and began to dance. It shattered into splinters,
one carving a salmon scar up my arm, five lines
black-starred with bark flecks, like musical
notation for my cry. I didn't feel my fall,

just heard my quiet. The white noise of my voice brought my
brother from inside our farmhouse,
and he carried me in, like I might have planned.

Dad made me stay inside, no worry in his tone,
just the same balm with which he'd read to us
from Genesis at breakfast, the world made and lost,
and I think he must have thought of the angel
in Eden, doing only good, when his chainsaw raced like a
killing wing, to cut the empty tree down
to its own bones, for me and for our fire that night.

An Invasion

We waited and waited, or by we,
maybe I mean I, to be invaded—
promised by Reagan, by Revelations,
by everything I thought we knew
about the Russians, even

by the way our play with
dump trucks and stick guns
always gave in to expectation,
a plateau I couldn't quite
play my way to-a truth.

So the first surge of worms
that brailled the catalpa tree,
army green, read enemy,
and I found out how to mount
that fantastic, cinematic attack
that brought no more hurt
than a shudder's worth--one rush
of my hand up the rough trunk,
and they cascaded into the pan
that transported them toward

the garage door, leaking dark
like a castle wall. On the porch floor,
cement swept empty, I made
ragged, prison grids of them,
but they scattered past patterns.

With the gold-colored bulldozer,
too rust-warted to be a toy,
I ran them down, found no
secrets, no future, just guts
the lima shade of their outsides.

But how great, I thought and felt
then, powered by fear, for
however many hours (if it
was even one), to see nothing
under a surface to hurt us,
nothing clutching a god or a plot
that might steamroll our freedom,
or our war. I don't remember
making any graves or pouring
them into the field of our yard.

I do remember, do I? Before
they were hurt, they made shapes
more shiveringly moving
to me than words. And then
I made them stop moving.

When I Was Baptized in Missouri Dirt

It stayed that same, steady
surrender of color, even dug
up and turned over, covering
the shovel in it, somehow
never quite sloughing off,
even as dry as it got, and as hot.

So, I like to look back
at that one rain that ran right into
the hour when our garden had
to be weeded, our norm,
our chore to do, us four
sort-of-city boys, moved
there from Ferguson, and one
of us found out how a molded
clod of that dirt, thick
enough to stick to itself
even as mud, flung,
would explode, and open up

the gray star of a crater, murder
on a white shirt.
And that was most of our hour,
all of us armed with as many
mud grenades as we needed,
none of us getting hurt,

feeling a little give in that dirt
as we ran on it, and, unlike
our pure savior, sinking in.

Echosystem

Nothing was made on our farm
that we didn't feed back to it,
either through the septic tank's baptism,
vectored and filtered,
or the composting of shells and hulls
in the omphalos,
I like to call it,
at the corner of our garden:

a nest-secure mess over the border
the gray gate made, where nature
took over in maybe many ways,
where our cows wandered
with that mix of dumb submissiveness
and impossible,
unstoppable propulsion,
both shown by how our ginger heifer

waited until we were out of sight
before pouring out her lowing,
in her tremolo, like a thicker
kind of wind
than the one that whined on in
through screens of trees
and splinter-furred fences,
and bulwarked small talk.

Then there was our garden,
a dark variety of yard
where growing things could
wind by their own
predictable will, with all our
watering,

our hacking, our turning and re-
turning the furrows
where stones kept growing,

turned up that dirt-burnished
fact in us, that the yield
would be just what it was,
and not what we wanted.
So, the compost heap,
where all these energies met
in that mystery of chemistry
we only needed to feed
and avoid, got whatever wouldn't
fit into our story,
and grew into what I somehow loved—
that plot we hadn't planned.
The luminous, lime-pale shoots
of some form of gourd wound out
like the limbs of a wild
spider freed from its pod body,

charging in slower motion
than can be seen
down the gold-brown
mound where manure
transubstantiated and
haunted straw.
Its leaves, I remember them best,
thick and sticky-silky
like a dragon's tongue,

frilled as rivers I'd
seen in pictures,
promising only to grow hope
and shelter whatever we

remembered there.
It got uprooted, had to,
like we would soon, again,
grown older, and even that
given back to it now--
how it was us, and wasn't.

Out of Our Farm's Odd Family of Birds

We had just the one duck
somebody, not me, named Qui Qui,
for the noise she made
or the one hoped for since, near me, she stayed
a violent kind of quiet
into which I projected the tension
of a power line or a star--

except when she tapped her beak,
orange as a hunter's reflector vest,
into our outdoor cats' tin pan of food,
not seeming to know her place in a chain
that made her prey, and therefore
fitting in, at least enough to suck up
one or two hard stars of it.

But she'd leave her place in the cat pack
to orbit our, or her, yard, to float
but by foot--not intent, not inspecting,
like her chicken cousins bug-hunting
in ranks by the oak trunks, not
stopping to nest like them,
but looking like a grounded cloud,

each stalk foot like lilac lightning
that could only paddle the grass,
no scorch in it but the one of numb touch.
I wouldn't qui to see if she'd quack back.
I tried to be like her,
with that stiff drift
in which she seemed always

to be her own, and never
to remember she was alone.

Our Farm's Warm Form of the Cold War

It wasn't one we had to win--our war.
Guard our half acre garden
so nothing could eat from it but us,
except when things did.
And I would find
wedge wounds in the tomatoes,

the sudden pinkish skin inside like mine,
the wrinkle-frilled edges too far
apart for a scar,
a sign of turtles otherwise invisible,
a sign to me to surrender,
or we risked further failure.

But one day, the three steel
threads of electric fence,
as perfectly stiff as a clef, stretched
around the perimeter.
In spite of the sparks it must have struck
in her nerves, our heifer

would put her weight against that
dam until it gave, and graze
the lettuce heads down to green-gray
carnations, the melons to abstract
jack o'lanterns, and whatever
else then went into our milk.

We would rebuild on summer
mornings, when the dirt we scratched at
got hotter than any wound I knew,
but before humidity ruined the wind,
and our war seemed so easy
to see, to lose, then to win again.

How Could the Tree Peepers be the Sources of Their Chorus?

Even when I'd see them,
finger pads living in cling
to wherever we weren't
supposed to find them,

the armpits between roots,
the steel-chilly
web-scribbled undersides of overpasses,
those moist voids they went
echo-hunting in,

one on its own would look too alien
to join the everyday noise of a season,
stuck in its own universe, shunt
from the one

of riding mowers sliding into home, of
the hayride after gametime,
of church, of work, of the verge
of nuclear winter we seemed to hover
just over, brutally routine,

leaving me like they must have felt—
slithery, other, needing to sing,
if only to breathe.

Autonomy

Our cats were hunters from birth—
first of safe places to nurse,
enough that they'd nuzzle a male's belly,
and find at least some sun heat
he'd soaked up from concrete.

Then, still kittens, bat-eared, scattered
enough to jump straight up
at just the rustle of a mole
under its built hill,
they'd prey on our hands,

claws caught in our skin,
legs trembly as web,
some something in their giant eyes
saying "play" in a way we knew,
that somehow told them, too.

Older, fuller in their fur,
molded to shadows and the dank lees
of oak trunks, they'd stalk
without a thought of us,
but did once plant what they caught

at our door

dying right on time.
They knew how to do it all,

and showed the new generation,
and our only role then: don't get bitten.

When Thunderclouds Rode Herd Above Our Yard

They made a wild, white field that seemed
to hold a hundred thunderstorms or more,
gray-white and germinating,
and I would see my way into them, when
I could never fly into the muscles
of the cumulonimbus or whatever they were
furrowed there, until their turning

toward storm formation, eye-gray
and overturned and undermined, churned
as if some cosmic worms in them
were burrowing and harrowing from within,
and I had time to follow them by sight
across the highway to that vanish
where the neighbors' woods walled them away.

Then there was the pause in which they just hung,
and, when I looked away for long enough,
like a plum they grew faintly
radiant bruises, then bled. But no, not
quite that quick, was it? That's just
how my memory edits its hesitation
out. No, this hiss came from everywhere:

rain saying its presence, its mass in
the vellum grass of our yard
and on whatever hidden citizens it held,
a kind of falling-also-rising sigh
answered by itself, no chorus,
no, a murmur-hum
until the air there pulsed and opalesced.

No, I didn't ever want that sort
of wet, that would mold
my clothes almost into my skin,

so I felt my own weight,
the one of son, of younger
brother, of accumulated faiths,
and so I'd run inside and wonder:

up above the by-then tiles of clouds,
who had tricked me into baptism?
And was it for my sins?
Or was it so I would not soil Him?

Our, Their Mirror

The cattle's water trough was dull steel,
and its level never sank,
at least when I looked into it,
even though the brown ground it sat on
seemed perpetually to be in a frieze
they'd made, hoof-roughened muck
of their own form of Expressionism.

The tank--their territory, not mine,
and I would not have put a hand into
their water even if they did yield it
and leave it a still mirror for the tree-
screened sky. It didn't seem clean to me,
though their tongues, brush-bristle-tough
and full of the wherever they'd been,
had maybe mainly lapped rain's traces

from the many root-hollows and gray
glades they'd wander in through the day
in our little woods that were too dense to dry
all the way. There, they'd blend in enough
to look like hidden spy satellites to my mind,
except the Guernseys, black-dappled but blank,
like all that water in their tank, under its

mirror face that anything might shatter and
reshatter. They never had long to live.
Hoping there was gentleness in that water
tank for them, in the shallow still waves
of its corrugated hull, free of meaning, and me.

Quintet for Our Chickens

For me, they lived four or five different lives,
first as bursts of goldenrod fuzz brought in brown crates
that we spread in a pen where we could see
through those dull steel honeycombs of our wire
at how they huddled in one yellow cloud
where the heat lamp stamped its glare, where their mother
figure laid, a plush, stuffed puppy given up by one of us,
just a stump leg jutting out of the mound
of them, that, with their nervous, constant chir-chir-chir
seemed like the underside of a sung hymn,
the fear there, the knowledge of being watched
but not what for, what future, by whose say.

Then we were carrying the pullets out,
one in each fist, like pistols but slung down, the
bent and whitened tridents of their claws
spread and clutching nothing up above,
knot knees not buckling, just as coldly still
as those wide, lentil-brown eyes, some of them
fluttering lids, some of them under combs
just coming uncovered, rubber-pink fins,
all their stump wings like those decorative doors
in our house, made to show rather than do,
some of their feathers still yellow, though paled
toward vellum, some blooming into plumage
that white, that delicate that it looked like foam
floating on their mercurial but still
selves, not moving. Somehow, they knew how to be held.

Then, in the dark chicken barn, they were their own,
the room hay-dusty, sewery with manure,
shut us out except for what we could not
avoid--the shimmy in along the walls

where the hens' nesting boxes were all nailed,
the check of one by one if left empty or
unguarded, and then the pluck of
one or two or so, most every morning,
pale but not cool, more like a white
coal than a burnt-out bulb, to pluck
and brush free of the filigrees
of straw plus chicken shit that sometimes clung,
and, in our yard, too, we let them have themselves,
the sane ones anyway, the new roosters
learning to crow dawn in at noon, squawk-wrong,
the hens who'd sit in our herb garden's dirt
in that shape of a wave made to move on.
They seemed to not see us except to run,
but when we had to hose out their--our barn,
I wondered if they knew, not where they were,
but whose.

By slaughter time, they came to seem like victims
to me, pale, shaking, hard to run down, but
not that hard, each one brought up, its head pinned
between a pair of nails stuck in a plank,
not Christlike in my mind, just curiosities,
how quick the life would leave them when Dad's axe
cut it out, then headless how their bodies
would hurtle into our yard, if we didn't
plant them in the trash can, clap the lid on,
and have my oldest brother hold it down,
the broken heartbeat of them wild inside.

Last are their carcasses, of course. I still
can feel the slippery zip of the pinfeathers
I tried to, couldn't, pluck out of chicken
skin that, plucked, looked like mine.
Can't remember what all I found inside,

but, yes, in that one, a space, a tiny sky
made of dark red I didn't see as blood,
because the gold yolks floating in it made
a cool, small constellation I could touch.

The Fold

As if our property was one shag rug
to be pulled into a rift and off the map,
it was split by a valley, hollow, shallow,
but with a bottom I could never see,
filled up with the billows and folds
of our yard, the massed, moist clippings
an acre of grass could make, harvested
by our mower, my older brother,
and all of us who'd rake and rake
it into drifts, less like warm snow
than dunes, especially when settled
in that valley. Into nothing but that

I might dive, knowing it would hold
my weight when I sank feet-deep,
risking the itch of the stalks caught in
my socks for that pillow feeling. But I
didn't know about the window the
grass had before the dumb ghost of
composting transfigured it to dirt,
and my dive one time fell outside
of it, into the phase my hand grazed
when I dug in just for more comfort.
Not viscous, not liquid, but thick muck

almost seeming to hum on my palm,
it ate at me, and I leapt up, left it
alone, that whole valley, from then on.
There was much to see outside of it,
the septic tank like a flyspecked
submarine drydocked for the Cold War,
the dark and glittery calligraphy of
barbed wire to mark a border

to our woods that held nothing in,
and the crumbling stump that would
stand in a moldy huddle of toadstools
until it simply gave and caved in,

since it had been colonized by wasps
who owned it like the valley did me—
because I would look into it, squint
and glance as if trying to deny it
and find it at once. Maybe it still
held a gift for me, as a past that sat
right where I wouldn't look, filled in.
There was no shadow of death in it,
and I had been told by the Bible, by
my mind, that I lived in that shadow.
Young, I felt like I could do nothing.
It left me with the gift of nothing to do.

CICADA
MEDITATION

If scatter was a pattern,
that's the one they made—no swarm,
no lines from hill or hive to sky.
They may have, must have come from the clusters
of thunderclouds when they lay
cocooned underground,
or constellations no one would see to trace.

But, out of it, they went where they fit,
some studding our oak's bark like beads,
free, unstrung,
others covering over the divots
of hail and the nail holes in our walls,

and the most isolated
simply settled anywhere, everywhere
else, making grass blades into cat tails,
sifting into the henhouse
like aliens hatched out of the blond
nesting boxes,
and infesting the feed, live mines.
They passed through our farm cats
almost whole.

*

They made my space their own, though,
as if they knew somehow
that I gave way to whatever I feared,
that even the tightening

of my skin by dried mud
felt a little hellish,
the brush of just one of them
on any of me. Our long lawn,
where I had played, became
their territory.

I was catapulted into battle patrol—
my imagination
magnifying their territory—
the summer-whitened
tines of grass jutting up
from the rune-writing of the brown
roots, easy to transform by daydream
into a supple jungle
where they waited, not patient,
just dumb.

But they waited
to be seen, to be touched,
and flutter under the toucher,
hoping not to have to live
in that shadow of a sky-annihilating
giant, one of my brothers,
maybe remembering the solid
shadow of the soil they'd left,
not to have to move again,
out of that sun, that country sun
that must have clung to their wings
like it did to my skin—sweat-heated,
honed by humidity into a lens,
absent and phantasmic.

Not far out of their shells,
they may have lived in that hope
not to be broken open
by something inside of them.

*

Anything undermining
routine was an invader,
and we engaged and engaged them
like dreams, always coming

and somehow almost calming,
highlights, at least in mind, cycling:

one brother severed their heads
like seeds he'd save,
that speckled the melon-red
bed of the wagon, and blended
with the little mortar craters
made by rust that couldn't
be painted over, not
counting them, not
even resentful, only
showing us our war,

and then my holding one,
holding off the blitz of jitters
its waxy, clammy armor
brought me, under the stutter
of water our outside spigot
shot when I wound the handle
past its last resistance,
and the whole insect came
undone, those glassy-white
water jets punching it
out of life and my hand,

and so many others crushed under
whatever we were.
We killed them with all we could be.
All shell
but the white wires of
some guts inside, they
could not be reduced past
that, even their eyes,
those tomato-red beads,
seemed to stay solid shreds,
so something of them,

crushed, kept up that act
of living, even of looking
back at us.

*

An exacting look back— what I have always hoped for
out of poetry? But my past is less
a place than a crumpled map
where the coordinates wander
by some order I don't know,
or a higher disorder, or
a war on the moment I'm in,
or grace's sometimes crazy-
seeming way. And I fear

that hidden in that army of undead
cicadas are the loved ones
I've sometimes run from,
sometimes left dead, the weight of it,
that only God should hold.

Why then
remember them,
reassemble every dismembered insect,
every lead-veined wing with its
pattern like a torn-down screen

in one of those country
doors, every nearly hollow
bullet-neat body, every eye
that had that impossibly small
dot of a pupil, to take in
as little of the light as it could
fly by—all torn down and made
into new earth
for however many decades

now, but it comes automatically—
imagination's hatching. Its army swarms.

How many loved ones have I
had and never even seen in any
human way, the many incubating
in the one routine, the heart-hurt, the stuff
everyone around me seems
to need in order to live, just
there to be walked over, or on?

There was Sarah,
fellow finalist for an award
in high school, and I knew
that she, like me, couldn't
get her head around it,
because of what her head held
against her, like mine, and
I would go around her because
she would hide behind
the library door and hold
herself the best she could.

Who have I given up—
what unloved ones?
Are they in me, an army,
like God was,
on my side?
Brothers, father, mother, Cold
War allies like the shy, shy
kids I'd silently, privately
side with in childhood,
cousins, humming swarms
of other presences in my
Perestroika post-divorce:
where are they in me?
Are they what stirs in there,

in that heart dirt I almost
can't stand to have sometimes?

*

I see one, composite cicada
that looks like almost all of them,
and I like to sum him up
as a mummy's thumb,
blackened like ivory is by time,
blunt at both ends,
face a button those eyes fit,
red, but this time, more like pinpricked
beads of blood, so say
the mummy was cursed only
to be folded in, to be devoid
on the outside, the bound
hide we see,
and buried underneath the living thing
his wings could look like a winding shroud,

shredded in symmetry; they lay there
mostly for ceremony. He roots
his penpoint feet in his territory, in
the site of his entire life.
The board I used as a toy sword
back then could have been laid
across the whole story of it–him. Them.
He seizes it, or her, whatever
he lives for, and that's it. Well,
he leaves a second shell, all
anyone could see of him.

Is it his heart in his eyes, those black specks,
when they target what he wants
or what his code leads to,

and finds by the guide that is his god
that flight, that mate, that bark gnarl
or twig to cling to, and there it is,
his narrow sort of a narrative,
an ordinary path to live?

*

I like to imagine that phantom
of a moment when some
chemical signals in them,
and however many thousand years
of stories in us,
got started, as a light apart
from the sun's, from the ones that seem
too practical, too devoted to running
centuries of routine, and also
that it looked more like fire than a star.

It may be bright violet,
and call dusk plum in that instant
cicadas make because they're made that way,
their voices cohere as that noise
that will only grow, will fill in the black gaps
that, all the cold year, had made
islands out of night sounds,

and that mass voice, yes, might be traced
into a purpose, a trance-inducing,
mating-facilitating thing,
but whatever; it lives; it lives in waves,
and however far in an imagined past
it is, I still feel I can ask its master,
and that I might hear an answer,
that I might still, in some part, be silent
or innocent enough to listen in.

*

Maybe I never felt a part of the country.
It seemed to want or need
to beat me, to turn my life there
into a surrender I could never give.
But that wasn't its fault, was it?
Maybe I wanted out of my head,
and out of that river
of nerves that everyone seemed to me
to ride toward God. Early on, then, I tried
to not stop holding
my breath, and to read my way free
of all that buzzing of wings, and even
at five, to find the tall girls to treat
like trees, if I could sit in their arms,
or stand in their fanned shadows.
In our neighbors, friendly and bent
into their labor all the time, in mind,
I saw some bulldozing of growing old,
where grace made a draining, grainy
kind of radiance, like a weak light breaking
on anyone broken who could still
somehow raise what was left of themselves
into it, and praise its maker in the pain
of giving praise, and repeat, day
by decimating day. Who did they see? Me?

*

What made me take such a savage
variation on a page
from the cicadas' book—a blank one
I wrote them, of becoming
a nothing, an absence, a noise far away,
that noise that stayed mine,
and I now see might be the dying kind?

Tithonus–I know this from
what seems like a summer's
worth of searching,
wanted what I wonder if I want,
to live forever, not as a way
to savor nature, but an escape
from the pain of aging,
and the gods made him age forever.

But in one version I dug up online,
they made him a cicada
whose buzz, a hymn to them,
would never end, like
the one they might have heard
after the same fluttering, splintering,
broken sorts of cicada hordes
as ours, in our Missouri Troy,
took over their groves.

Was it then
an unlistenable, thankfully ungranted
request for death?

*

The wake of a past classmate
was in that same part of the country
as our former farm. I tried, one more time,
to read his face.

But it was just a mask, a husk;
he'd blown the soul out of it,
and the undertaker had already
drained away all but the exoskeleton,
but it looked like it had sat vacant,
like he had been buried even when
I knew him, frame to a seam,

and the violet of its colored eyelids,
showed, and shows, only spent shell.

What made it so that he wasn't saved
but I am, I don't know. But because
that something in me laminates
the question in imagination,
I nearly hear, under the flutter
of talk attacking the loss as we sat
with it in the brown main room
of the funeral home, old Troy Missouri
making that punishing kind of a hush
out of summer heat and that wind
that seems to only end and end,

but under that, and breaking it
by climbing, the clicks like locks
of cicadas making an incantation,
not singing a mass on purpose,
but just lost, and not yet able
to see the daylight they play in.

If I could have stayed later
and mourned more, I would have.
But I can imagine, I try,
the cicadas seeding those Missouri trees,
mourning for me.

*

I've never tried to return, but I do
believe I found a dumb kind of love that
I might pray my way back to again, for
the cicada nymphs that didn't fit in:

they had that faint, bright yellow
almost like butter or custard, but brighter,

as if lit just a little from within,
that made their eyes look dark, and
their wings magnified it, made it glint,
and they'd hold the bark hard, but
if pulled, would surrender, sit

in wind and use those wings, or
sit on my fingers like light that wouldn't hurt.

Can this incubate into a metaphor for grace—
that I couldn't feel their weight,
only the faith that they wouldn't fly away?

Is that what almost lifts me when I pray?

OUR DARK
BACK ACRE

The Tin Can Cemetery We Inherited

The places we should have never
gone, I and my brothers went, even
dove into, then the ones made
for meditation, if not excavation,
we'd speed past, at least I did,
past that squared, bone-gray cage
of two by fours, easy to visit,

showing through its fat gaps a sort of hoard postmodern
archaeologists could have swarmed.
We weren't, though, so there they
stayed, tin cans all rusted over years
to that same chestnut shade,
not the toad color of mud

in our part of the country, or
holding any hint of any other
critter, but maybe the shade
of a hide we'd never see--real
color of a brontosaurus--or the
insides of the trees of our woods.
That empty cemetery of cans

stayed too warped in scallop shapes
to look like a junk mosaic, but, settled
into one rough stratum too flat
to do anything like cushion a crash,
they simply waited to be taken in by
patient eyes that might have
savored their rust the color of the hemi-

sphere of Mars turned against sun,
and under that red shadow found

maybe the faint angels of labels
to tell us what was eaten, and hint at
by whom. But we couldn't see our farm
as Eden if anyone had been there
before. And we fought that metallic
past with that weapon of ignoring
carrying us, like the plush, stuffed
horse we'd brought out of the cold
war, the one we'd seen on the Zenith
tv in shades of gravel gray. Could it
all, that can dump, have been assembled
into an armor, or the air-marrowed,

hollow body of a robot like in books?
Why didn't we bury that layer in ours?
If "ubi sunt" fits this poem, oh where
were our curiosities? What about a
deft zest for mystery, pastime of the lost?
Were we? Lost? Or was it just me?
And am I coming home only slowly

to a space created before my mind,
and filled with less-than-epic relics
to sift with the stick of an unrhymed
line, for what, under the rust of a numb
I needed even then, might shine?
If we had taken time, we might have
learned so thoroughly who we were not.

The Treed Reef

Days, I tried to say I was afraid,
and hide behind that,
away from the old boards
that made for a bad ladder
up the trunk of one of our oaks

into the, not a tree house
at that point,
picked apart by my
brothers, the hunters, but a
treed, wood reef,
making shaking walkways
out over the open ground where they might safely be able to
fall, only for one story or so, although
I knew I would, if I did try

that flight, be guided toward
the stick splintered into a
white stake, or turned head
over end to break my neck
like an umbrella plant stalk.

Or I might even be blown away by
a sudden tornado, a Soviet
spy satellite, or say a laser,
tools of my private, violent
god, not theirs, who

loved them enough to hover, while mine sat waiting
to come hunting. Love
was the one blood trail,
and family the only

wound that grew it.
But family was my deity,
so at last I went up just once,
more fearful of saying
no than letting go,

holding and hiding
my tiny pride like an iron kite,
while my brothers were holding
and pulling my forearms
that worked like white ropes,

and I did, I stayed long enough to
get that giant's eye view:
the boards a walkable web
across ash-black branches,

ground made strange
in their frame, way more like
fur than dirt, and our air
holding just itself in
between, until I could

finally, briefly see it
holding me.

Gone On Home

I have tried to find elegies in the Iliad,
in those lean spans after the warriors have
been offered up to us as extinct
family names, after that dissection-precise
violence Homer, if there was one, wrote, no,
spoke. Once, I swear those elegies were

there, like the scurf or snarls of saints'
once-radiant hair in the cold gold casing
of Pope's translation where no blood runs,
rather, wounds bloom purple as falchions,
never spears, are buried there. There, once,
I swear I saw the stories of their home

countries—harvests, farms, not so much
wives or daughters, but sons, of course, poured
into view. . . . But I can't navigate back to those
lines. Is that sad? What about how the Troy
Missouri woods laid its, or their, nameless
claim to pets and possessions we knew were

ours—cats we'd named, and hadn't Adam
gotten dominion by giving names? No woods
went on the deed for our property. It was ours.
But it claimed and claimed. Frost—was he
wrong? Had we always been the land's?
But he'd read it for a president. Wouldn't God,

if not poets, mold it all to our brief needs,
weed away all those shadows that would never
leave completely, but grow every day to the same
height, then, envy of the Soviet Union, colonize
our bedrooms at night? We wouldn't look too
hard for what the woods took from us,

because of that understanding—twin of
wonder, is it? We knew it got its due. No
mountain lions in it now, mastodons only
in partial fossils, fur like circuitry in the rock
under the bedrock. But it got its due.
Our farm cats who vanished in it, even the one

we found shot and we buried in our own,
mowed territory, we wouldn't have looked for
harder than it looked after them. When
the neighbor who cared for the creatures
we considered ours had to bury the cat, then
calf who died, he made one or two cairns,

stones piled like a sacrifice after all. Have we
grown past that romantic twist in taste,
where we search for our own roots in the
organism such a forest is, this deep in the gene,
an epic with such depth? Well, do we need to
meet the roots of these sorts of trees? Will

they meet us one of these days, grow through
our bark, the trunks of our caskets, and
hold us like we'd never let them do?

Harvesting the Darknesses Between Our Trees

The musk of a black walnut,
shucked into the dark part
or worn down through it
into the corrugations of shell,

shell's fingerprint or Milky Way
spill of whorls, I'd feel sharp
at my fingers, chapped that
late in our farm year.

The musk blooms more than
rises in my mind, not stale
sweat, but not quite fresh,
not a pine kind of spice,

but like a crushed handful
of all the woods could hold,
perhaps its past. It would hit,
that scent, it would hint at a sting,

and they did--we'd play grenades.
They were just a little brighter
than that Allied kind of green.
Finding one in that Sargasso

space where manure turned
into boot-clutching mud, who
could resist a wide, side-arm arc
of just one, at a fellow hunter

of a brother? It might hit quilting
of a hunting coat, or the ultimate goal—
skin it could sting with a pink disk.
But whatever the war there,

we'd have to come with buckets
loaded so they rattled like dice
or "bones" the outlaw kids called them,
or actual knucklebones wicking

that iguana skin husk around the nut
away, if it had rotted soft enough
to wart and split with a stiff grip.
Shucking them had that slick

satisfaction of taking off a mask,
even though the work had only
passed the midpoint, if that—even
though we'd spread them like seeds

to crack under our car tires and
take up the work after that
of eating what seemed not
made for human taste. It was

as if they had tasted too much
themselves already to be objects,
had soaked up blood of our dark
back acre--its rain, its decay,

its bitter little mysteries.
But we ate anyway—they were free.

Our Wild Animals

When the cats went out hunting,
we didn't see them, not even a gleam
of fur barred by high, mouse-loved grass
there between fences, close to the house.

Even when we owned a couple dozen
they would all erase themselves,
as if they didn't know we owned them,
and seemed to be able to disappear

without even leaving us, at least me,
the memory of them. I would not spot
the lack of them in my field of vision,
with its mix of trees and light-eating,

nameless to me, colonies of scrub,
where my mind would pour the stories
I'd been reading—fears gone feral there.
Probably, I now see, my cat Sadie

with her slate pelt and bone-gray
eyes, burrowed through those shallow
shadows, paws soft enough to bluff
rodents into the open,

and the obsidian one, with the half-
mask of two or three of fire's duller colors
ablaze in a cool dull way on his face,
could push further into their warrens

and snap with his yawned jaws,
a body oscillating, squeaking, breaking
the raw stalk neck. What a quiet, violent life
they and all the others led, to feed,

to be themselves, at least until
at that rattle of cat food in the tin pan,
we'd watch the woods shake them loose,
each streaking from some form of nowhere

to gather at its brim, their tails radiating
from it, eating its middle back to shining,
almost as civilized as us at our supper.
But I must have wondered, in that numb,

smothered way of a nightmare
hunkered under morning prayer,
if they put on that scene to give us peace,
let us live out that "master" act,

and I remember, with a little, mental
tremble, opening the door that led to
their territory, their porch to see some
of them laying astray, like broken stained

glass panes, around a rabbit, half-grown,
cocoa coat and no wound we could see,
hunched against its own, growing cold,
in its knot eyes with that something past hurt.

We tried to save it—that was who we were.
It died, they ate, and afterward they purred.

Baptism on Our Terms

When we would swim in Lincoln Lake,
sometimes a faint rain came,
a gray-white haze between us and the trees
at that unmanned end,
but it had no more impact than
a phantom's up above,
since the clouds didn't lose
any of their blue-gray plumes,
giving not so much as a quill
to the squall. But it made a more

ghostly show on the broken-open,
owl-brown faces of the waves,
already muddied and slapped into
little hills by all of us milling kids,
the drops raising fluid goosebumps.
Then, if it roared
into that sudden country
of a summer storm,
blowing open pores in the water
that wind widened into craters before

it healed closed, closed by that inevitable
weld of wave to wave
that I saw with a kind of lost
but still-open hope, as if it all had almost
shattered to let me walk
safely along the bottom, I would try
to let it carry me, guiltily.
Too cosmic and mucky at once to me,
all filled in, too close to bottomless,
too unable to be seen through,
like everyone I knew--I still had to walk

into it, breath held for just a duck
out of sight of the oldest brother who told us
all, "if you get underwater, the rain can't hit you."

What felt dirtiest, and most alluring—
that gap where the fluffy
chafe of the mud
that had grown like smoke at my ankles
in the shallows, that had turned
invisible when i had wandered out
up to my shoulders, here at the drop-off,
thinned and went colder
before disappearing with the ground,

leaving only waves and their cold,
undercurrent roots, along with anything
I couldn't see, my mind conjuring
the body of one of the condemned men
our favorite reverend had
raised in my imagination,
out of the sermon with the most brimstone,
to noose and hang from a rafter,
crafted out of an absent god's anger,

and my mind's pine for some
self-inflicted sin like masturbation
or contemplating communism,
white marbles of his knuckles
glowing just under my madly paddling feet,
kelp-tendoned jaw clapping
in its own, silent current, with the one
kind of penitence I felt--
weak, too late, like a stick
I'd try to ride toward shore.

I knew my only way was what I felt,
so I adored the turn back, out of the rain's wake,
the paddle that looked and felt like a last gasp, all
my limbs working too hard,
my breath and its words part water,
for that thrash into the bright part,
where it went hip-deep, and shallower,
until my feet got cut off at the ankles by waves I had made.

And then I could look back into that lake,
feeling its last mist falling down on me,
but not get immersed in its mystery.

Our Dark Back Acre

There was no alone in those woods,
I thought, because of what I brought in:
so many fear-veneered hopes of ghosts,

from the one of Bluebeard maybe-chased
by the white wraiths of his killed wives
to our pets I had never learned the grieving

of, that might come rottenly glimmering
into that wet, root dark, hunting me or
at least my heart, or the holy, was it ghost

or spirit that I felt might lodge like some
prayer-honed arrowhead in that baby
fat I couldn't seem to shame away?

I took them as far in there as I could,
those fears, that were not feral after all,
or not enough to grow in our dark

back acre, where the leaves that had been
shed were darkened to the color of tar
and clung to each other, made into

those tattered batwings by wet rot,
were their own ghosts, where the scaly,
oily, alien hands of umbrella plants

tangled at my ankles, and all those old
oak trunks broken open, heartwood
bored and mandibled into coils that

looked mechanical and intestinal at

the same time, showed the eye-white
shine of the wet-shelled bugs that

somehow knew to vanish when I'd
crash through, and then the dead I
knew seemed nothing like mine,

as they'd rise and sigh, cohering only
momentarily a branch sinewed with a
shadow turned a hand--of course,

it must have been the one ancestor
already an angry ghost in the tan-
cream photo, whispering with

mummified vocal cords the curse
placed on boys who didn't get their
verses memorized. And the creak

within a living trunk fit with the
muscling of its bole to bring back
that kid shot dead in the city,

who'd only wait, who'd only silent-
cry for the right playmate there
in that dead rain of a dripping

canopy. It seemed to me like an
anointing oil, a haunted kind
that marked me like those who had

only died just enough to stay far
out past our house, hungry for company.
And there they were, the ones out

of Reverend Ken's sermon, hung
no more, lurking but rocking in that dim
gray-green stain of shade.

No creatures were here that I could
see, or were we all creatures here?
Were all of us living things alike

in the red eyes of a mad god
who'd found a way in this Missouri
dark to let us burn from within?

"It don't show and if it don't show
it ain't there" they'd say ...
wouldn't they, those inner voices

I could not, when back in weak
daylight, let out by mouth?
But when I look back, so many living

things were there with me. I was not
what I thought, or what I felt, or what
held those feelings in a dark back acre

of their own. But I do find I want
a dark back acre to vanish in
sometimes,

and a God who made shadows

must not mind.

Blood of the Woods

If those woods of ours ever bled,
it didn't run underground.

It lacquered the burn-brown leaves
that matted and paled the grass

like hands where they fell.
It kept the dirt, that stayed in shade,

that kind of moist with no luster,
the kind that ate light and gave

only the cologne of something
stuck becoming not quite ripe,

not quite rotten. It dimmed
roots, too, of trees I could only

climb by the eye. It fit my soles
and toes, too animal to be

baptismal, making my feet
part black as bark. It blushed

the banished cans with rust,
hung fungus like stained lace

on downed boughs, upholstered
trunks with crocodile scales

of lichen. Part groundwater, part
cloud, it would sit on my skin,

alien, then, as only that good kind
of blood could, it would run in.

ACKNOWLEDGMENTS

Gratefully acknowledged are the following publications where poems appeared in earlier versions:

"When I Discovered Sacrifice By Fire," *Massachusetts Review*

"Faller," *Spillway*

"An Invasion," *Plume*

"When I Was Baptized in Missouri Dirt," *swamp pink*

"Echosystem," *Birmingham Poetry Review*

"Out of Our Farm's Odd Family of Birds," *Ecotone*

"Our Farm's Warm Form of the Cold War," *swamp pink*

"How Could the Tree Peepers be the Sources of Their Chorus?," *AGNI*

"Cicada Meditation," *At Length*

"Our, Their Mirror," *Copper Nickel*

CHAD PARMENTER is a Missouri-based poet and writer. His work has appeared in publications including *Best American Poetry, Harvard Review, Kenyon Review,* and *At Length.* His writing about poetry has appeared in publications including *American Poetry Review* and *Memorious.* His chapbook *Weston's Unsent Letters to Modotti* won the Snowbound Chapbook Contest at Tupelo Press. His book *Batmanticism* was published by In Case of Emergency Press. His plays *The Rat Trap* and *The Short Knight* were featured in the Comedies in Concert series of the University of Missouri, where he received his PhD.

www.ingramcontent.com/pod-product-compliance
Lightning Source LLC
Chambersburg PA
CBHW030513130626
46549CB00007B/2972